"Loving Leah: A Legacy Revealed by a Woman Unloved"
Copyright 2009 by Sylvia Page

Published: October 2011

ISBN 9780615522760

All Rights Reserved

Printed in United States of America

All scripture references adapted from the Holy Bible, New International Version, copyright 1999 (Holman Bible Publishers)

Acknowledgements

The following persons have enhanced the content of this devotional:

- God the Father, my Lord and Savior Jesus Christ, and the Holy Spirit: I am eternally grateful for your unconditional love, for counting me worthy of purpose, power and your perfect peace
- My parents, especially my mother Ada, who instilled in me precepts of faith, love for the arts, a strong work ethic and compassion for others
- Bishop Michael Lee Graves and Lady Eleanor Graves of Temple Church in Nashville, Tennessee who loved me as extended family, encouraged my dreams, guided by example and taught me how to bring God's word alive in my life
- My children Robert and Dorian, who never fail to encourage me, love me and make me laugh. You and Camille confirm God's kindness to me
- My grandchildren, a constant joy to my soul, evidence of God's grace toward me
- God-sisters Toby, Debbie, Elizabeth, Sherrie who weathered several storms with me
- Pastors Darrell Drumwright, Victor Wynn & the Temple family for emotional support, sound teachings and inspiring me toward excellence,
- Dr. Chris Jackson & Dr. Vanessa Barbour, your editing/technical skills have been a blessing.

Forward

This book is written to all women, whether single, married, widowed, or those hoping to marry, any woman who has ever allowed emotional love to over-ride her good sense. While we may never meet, that does not diminish the fact that we are sisters by nature. If you have ever loved somebody to the point that you cannot get through the day without hearing their voice several times or if you have ever felt insecure, disconnected, fretful or anguished over how much your husband or significant other cares about you.....*then I wrote this book for you!*

As a woman, I understand your desire for affirmation, affection, and companionship. I know what you feel as you walk through a shopping mall alone or maybe join your girlfriends at a restaurant or movie, only to absent-mindedly begin to observe the couples nearby holding hands. Lastly, if you are normally an intelligent person, yet find yourself thinking or acting irrationally or just plain stupid, this book is written *straight from my heart to yours!*

Dedications

This book is dedicated to:

the memory of my mother and brother, both of whom were raised in foster care. Their faith and musical talents placed them in the midst of stars, then and now,

the memory of my father, who was proud of me but gone too soon,

the "Loving Leah" study group, whose stories still inspire me: Cheryl, Clemestine, Darlene, Juliaett, Kimberly, Latoya, Lemon and Peggy,

the three men I loved as best I could, *while I could.* Through you, God drew me to Him.

Table of Contents

Acknowledgements..................................page 2

Forward..page 3

Dedications..page 4

1. Glancing Back at the Future...............page 6

2. Deception Comes at a Cost................page 14

3. A Change is Gonna Come...................page 21

4. God Sees and He Cares......................page 30

5. By Virtue of Her Virtues....................page 41

6. Hoping Against Hope..........................page 52

7. Boundaries Are Best..........................page 58

8. Faith is the Substance.......................page 66

9. Sex For Mandrakes............................page 73

10. Covenant Protection........................page 79

11. At Last, the Honor...........................page 84

Loving Leah

A Legacy Revealed by a Woman Unloved

It has been stated that a woman was created with two internal voids. One void only her heavenly father can fill. The other void is for her man. I once heard a television evangelist say, "It is often not our choices that bring us stress, it is the consequences." Even in my own life that statement has been proven true. It is comforting to know that our life manual, the Holy Scriptures, records the first scenarios where human beings come face to face with *consequences*. It doesn't matter whether thousands of years ago or yesterday, whenever our selfish nature dominates, it only takes a split second to make choices based on an immediate craving or concern.

Before visiting the leading lady of this devotional, I invite your attention to Genesis Chapter 25. There begins a provocative story of desperate housewives, cravings, choices and consequences which were long lasting and life changing for one unique family. As we peek into Isaac's personal life we discover that at 60 years of age, he fathered twin sons, Esau and Jacob by his wife Rebekah. (Genesis 25: 21-26). Several years later, Esau encountered his twin brother Jacob as Esau returned home exhausted from a long day of hunting. When enticed by Jacob to trade for a bowl of stew, Esau's temporary craving (his hunger) overrode his better judgment. He traded something far more valuable than a bowl of stew. He traded his precious birthright! We can equate this to several athletes and other famous people of today. Celebrities often get enticed by the glitz and glamour associated with their celebrity status. They often decide they must possess whatever momentarily fulfills them but usually at a very high cost.

I wonder can you identify a time when someone or some situation influenced you toward a hastily made decision? Or, rather than an external influence, have you ever struggled with an inner enticement to yield your boundaries with the belief that you'd gain <u>more</u>? Use the space below to describe the situation and outcome.

Much later, father Isaac makes a family-altering decision, after falling victim to an intricately planned deception hatched by his own wife, *Rebekah.* You see, the stew and birthright incident resulted in a serious disagreement between Jacob and Esau. The situation was aggravated by Esau marrying two women which *were a source of grief to Isaac and Rebekah*

(Genesis 26). Rebekah decided to take matters into her own hands and resolve this personal grievance she held against Esau. To top it off, Jacob was Rebekah's 'favorite son'. She hadn't planned on Esau getting angry enough to want to kill Jacob! Once she overheard Esau's plan of revenge however, Rebekah confided in Jacob, convincing him to leave home for his own safety.

Mother Rebekah resorted to manipulating Isaac rather than owning up to her interference. She didn't want to look foolish or 'in the wrong'. Can you relate? Instead, she reminded her husband of the disobedience and distress Esau had caused by marrying <u>two</u> foreign Hittite women. Rebekah complained to Isaac that if Jacob should <u>also decide</u> to marry outside their culture, "her life would not be worth living." Why? It's quite probable that Esau's wives intimidated Rebekah, held different standards, challenged her status, or maybe they were an embarrassment to her within their community.

Or, there could have been issues of jealousy between the in-laws. All we know for sure is that Rebekah chose to get her favorite son out of town quickly, rather than confessing to her husband the integral part she played in deceiving everyone.

There's no doubt that Rebekah was a devoted wife and mother. Yet, she lost focus and displayed behaviors that <u>were not</u> part of a faith-filled life.

<u>Reflections:</u>

Have you ever convinced yourself there was a good motive to cover up something, only to have that small problem "blow up" into a much larger incident? Below, briefly describe the situation and outcome.

On some level, most women can relate to the anxieties and fear that gripped Rebekah. Take time now to 1) identify any emotion that causes you to think or act sinfully, and 2) confess to the Holy Spirit that you need help so you can respond with wisdom next time (James 1:5).

Was 'jealously' one of the emotions you recognized in Rebekah (and perhaps yourself)? If not resolved, jealousy usually has an extremely negative impact. Not only was Rebekah probably jealous about the influence Esau's wives had over him, she could also have been frustrated about her husband preferring Esau over Jacob (which was her favorite).

Another strong impulse motivating Rebekah could have been her need 'to control the decisions/behaviors of others'. Do you know any women who struggle with that issue now (perhaps unaware)? How has their <u>need to control</u> impacted their employment or family life?

While the years passed and Isaac became increasingly feeble, he relied on his eldest son to provide food for the family. After hunting, Esau was often expected to prepare Isaac's favorite meal. During one such occasion, Isaac, being extremely ill, decided to bless Esau before he died (Genesis 27:40-5). Rebekah, as stated earlier, was hovering nearby (with her own agenda). She seized the opportunity to get the covenant blessing (intended for Esau), switched to her favorite son, Jacob.   Scripture states that Jacob tried "to get himself off the hook" from his mother's elaborate scheme, which was for Jacob to imitate Esau, thereby tricking Isaac (Genesis 27:11-12). Jacob initially objected, worried that his mother's deception would bring a curse <u>upon his own head.</u> Rebekah replied that <u>she</u> would absorb any potential 'curse', in his stead. That flimsy reassurance was all it took for Jacob to conspire with his mother! They defrauded Esau out of the special blessing Isaac meant for him.

Rebekah didn't consider Esau being so outraged as to want his brother dead (a consequence).

Identify any incident (involving family, work, friends) which caused such distress that you considered doing <u>whatever it took</u>, to reduce the pressure, disappointment or level of anxiety you experienced. Did you conspire with others or compromise <u>your values</u>? If you felt any uneasiness or lingering regret then or now, you can confess and repent....right now!

<u>Pause and Pray</u>

"Forgive me oh Lord, forgive me the sins of my past, the sins of my soul and the sins of my body. Forgive the sins which I have done to please myself and the sins which I've done to please others. Forgive me for idle sins, forgive me for my serious and deliberate sins and the sins which I have labored so hard to hide from others, that I have hidden them from my own memory. Remove now the burden of guilt and let me feel

and know the assurance of your pardon. Direct what I shall be and help me always to walk in the commandments and ordinances and follow until my life's end in the footsteps of Jesus Christ, in whose strong and precious name I pray."

Chapter 2

The trusting Isaac, never considering that his beloved wife and younger son would plot to undercut his authority, laid his hands on and mistakenly assigned the covenant blessing (inherited from Abraham) on to Jacob who enters his father's tent, disguised in Esau's garments. Later (at Rebekah's prompting) Isaac instructs Jacob to leave quickly and travel to the land of Haran to secure a wife from within Laban's family (Jacob's uncle, brother to Rebekah).

Apparently, this was Jacob's first experience with being on his own for such a long time. What

a hasty transition for Jacob! Imagine the sights, sounds and thoughts which infiltrated his mind during that journey of about 500 miles.* Bible scholars believe Rebekah also traveled the same distance many years before when she was selected to become Isaac's wife (a coincidence?).
*Higgs, Liz C., Slightly Bad Girls of the Bible, (2007).

Reflections:

As you recall a previous trip of your own into 'unfamiliar' territory, were you reluctant, sad, excited, fearful or all of those? If the trip was long enough, were you able to contemplate your previous choices/behaviors, as well as, what lay ahead? I certainly remember one long journey as I relocated from one state to another. I accepted a new job about 2000 miles away from family, church members and close friends. I told everyone I was offered a great salary (which I was). I didn't tell anybody that the decision to relocate was based primarily on my yearning to be close to a handsome and seductive man to whom I was emotionally attached. He didn't ask me to follow him, but I clung to the hope that once I <u>proved to him</u> how much I cared, he in turn would choose me over others he spent time with. When reality finally set in, I was left feeling humiliated and hurt. Sisters, when a man <u>shows</u> you he does not share your emotions, *<u>please believe him!</u>*

Let's take a minute now and reflect back on big brother Esau (Genesis 27), the so-called "wronged brother" who Jacob ran from. At first glance, we don't notice major problems between Esau and his parents. There is no record of a major incident until Esau exchanged his birthright for a bowl of stew, right?   Sorry...wrong answer. A closer scrutiny of Genesis 26:34-35 is needed. Initially, it is easy to feel sorry for Esau, until his flagrant acts of rebellion are put under the spotlight. Esau was a good son pretty much; however, he disobeyed <u>and disappointed his</u>

<u>parents in a major way.</u> At age 40, rather than being mature and honoring his parents, he had lusted after *and married two women* outside his family's culture/nationality. Esau disregarded cultural norms and boundaries. He made choices which reflected "I'm my own man, my parents are old-fashioned. I'm grown, independent and I'll marry whoever I choose."

<u>Reflections:</u>

Can you recall an act of dissension or rebellion you committed either against a long-standing rule or authority figure in your life, or perhaps against a godly precept? Did you learn a lesson right away or much later?

Evidently, Esau's mother felt hurt and frustrated for a long time. After all, Rebekah had been married for 20 years before bearing children. She probably tried to reason with Esau and having failed, she tried to "keep the peace". Esau's <u>two foreign wives may have provoked</u>

their mother-in-law by ignoring her instructions or laughing at the family's religious beliefs.

Perhaps she struggled with feeling 'pushed aside', since her oldest son disregarded tradition and married women she and Isaac labeled <u>heathen</u>.

It is also probable that whenever household 'squabbles' erupted, Esau sided with his wives, rather than his mother. As a counselor, I've seen how hard it is for Christians (and non-believers) to overcome <u>resentment.</u> That particular emotion can be long lasting. If left unresolved, resentment breeds bitterness. Subsequently, when Esau 'despised his birthright' (swapping it for the stew); in Rebekah's eyes, Esau had "added insult to injury". She angrily decided to execute some revenge to halt Esau's reckless behavior. Rebekah did not however, fully weigh the potential, long-term <u>consequences.</u>

Pause and ponder:

How can you relate to Rebekah's state of mind? What other options should she have considered to avoid lying to her husband and provoking Esau's decision to kill his brother Jacob? What would you have done?

Much later, after Jacob left home journeying to his uncle Laban's house, Esau had a change of heart (Genesis 28:6-9). Part of Isaac's blessing to Jacob included instructions that he would not marry Canaanite women. This is what Oprah Winfrey would call Esau's "ah-hah moment". Esau recognized and sincerely regretted dishonoring the beliefs of his parents. No formal apology is recorded in Genesis; however, Esau tried to make amends through his third marriage. He chose for his next wife, Maholalth, a daughter of Ishmael (Abraham's first son by Egyptian slave, Hagar). Yes, you read correctly. Esau's first cousin became his third wife!

If Jacob had not been compelled to leave home, do you think Esau would have corrected his own acts of rebellion? Describe in your own words how something good can result from a bad situation.

I hope you can identify that there are several kin-folks in this family who had struggles between doing the right thing and doing what 'felt right' at the time (depending on the current influence). Sisters, this emotional conflict has existed since the beginning of recorded time. Humans are created with three innate levels of being: the physical, the emotional and the spiritual. We are not always the best decision makers, right? So, rather than reacting in haste or out of wounded pride, Christian women must discipline themselves to seek godly wisdom and understanding for <u>all</u> issues of life. Before we proceed, join me please in reflecting on an inspiring passage of scripture:

"Get wisdom, get understanding; do not forget my words or swerve from them, do not forsake wisdom, and she will protect you; love her, and she will watch over you. Wisdom is supreme; therefore get wisdom. Though it cost all you have, get understanding. Above all else, <u>guard your heart</u>, for it is the wellspring of life." (Proverbs 4: 5 – 7, 23)

Chapter 3

That scripture passage in Proverbs 4 was addressed to males/sons. Yet, I believe it's also very relevant for women of all ages because we often associate our strong <u>emotions</u> with 'truth'.

Earlier, I shared that I once relocated my family, took a new job in another state with the secret hope of being close to a man I was deeply attached to. He didn't quite feel the same way (to put it mildly). In fact, I wonder if he'd even recognize me today if we ended up across the room from each other. So what enticed me to alter my life and chase after him? My emotional attachment was extremely strong, and my physical yearning for him was poignant. To be honest, those lustful *feelings* were the core of my decision making. I didn't fully consult God for wisdom, I kept praying for God to let me have my <u>fairytale.</u> Once I made up my mind that my love for him would eventually win him over toward loving me, I was off and running....*right into a brick wall!*

As previously mentioned, before Jacob and Esau were born, another story is told of how Abraham's servant traveled a distance of 500 miles, searching for a wife for his younger son Isaac (Genesis 24). Another woman, hoping to live her own "fairytale" left her close-knit family and traveled back with the servant to become the wife of a husband selected for her. Of course,

Rebekah became that wife. Now in Chapter 28, largely due to her deceit, Rebekah's favorite son Jacob begins his own lonely journey from Beersheba to Haran. I am reminded of lyrics from a gospel song: "If it had not been for the Lord on my side, where would I be, where would I be?"

Jacob rested one night and had a fretful, compelling dream (Genesis 28:11-17). That vision reaffirmed the same Lord which had made a covenant with his ancestors, was now making a covenant with Jacob. Because of this spiritual encounter which changed his heart, Jacob's personal relationship with the Lord took on a new depth...a deeper significance. I believe Jacob repented of his part in cheating Esau and the Lord forgave him immediately. Jacob moved from the 'religion' of his parents, to his own 'personal relationship' with the Lord. This is God's ultimate goal for all of us who call upon His name. Infused with gratitude and respect, Jacob anointed the spot where he had dreamed. He vowed that if the Lord would be with him, protect and provide for him, and return him safely to his home, then the Lord would be his God and all that God gave him, Jacob would give back a tenth (tithe).

Spiritual Truth:

Whenever God has a purpose for you, He may decide <u>not</u> to change the outward circumstance.

He can however, surely bring about a specific change <u>within you!</u>

Reflection:

Can you recollect a time when God, despite your pleadings to Him, allowed an unpleasant circumstance to <u>remain</u> while He changed you (from inside)? Were you or were you not able to grow in your understanding of how God allows "all things to work together for your good?"

Jacob finally completes his trip and arrives exhausted but safely into Haran. There he talks with shepherds who say his uncle Laban's daughter **Rachel** is approaching with her sheep. They explain to Jacob their usual procedure for watering the flocks from the nearby well. Once Rachel arrived, Jacob was so overwhelmed to see "kinfolk", or perhaps in an attempt to impress Rachel with his strength, he rolled the stone away from the well so Rachel's sheep could be watered first. He then kisses Rachel (Genesis 29:11) and cries out loud.

Reflections:

The Bible is not specific, but what could have prompted Jacob's emotional outburst? Do you think he was genuinely grateful that his long journey was over and God had guided him safely to his destination, or do you believe Jacob actually "fell in love at first sight"?

Many women, due to being abused and misused, may no longer believe in "love at first sight". Personally I think Jacob could have been totally infatuated with Rachel's physical appearance. Maybe as the young men use to say: Rachel was "a brick house". Whatever you decide, the scriptures state that by the end of Jacob's first month with his relatives, he <u>was in love</u> with Rachel.

Laban asked Jacob to set his own wages for his labor. Jacob voiced his willingness to work 7 years in exchange for Rachel's hand in marriage. Once those years were complete, Jacob of course was extremely anxious to claim Rachel as his bride (Genesis 29:21). Laban gathered all the neighbors and made a celebration feast. Then, under cover of darkness, it was not Rachel that was presented as Jacob's long-awaited bride but her older, much less attractive sister, **Leah.**

It appears Jacob didn't acclimate himself to the traditions of his new region. Yet, why did Laban treat Jacob as he would a stranger? Why didn't he clarify with Jacob years earlier that their custom was for the elder daughter to be married first?

Reflections:

Have you ever experienced a similar situation where you felt really sure of something or somebody, then much later were stunned to discover you <u>did not have all the facts</u>? Write down at least two emotions you experienced:

_____ and _____.

Now I don't know about you, but I can quickly think of some guys from my old neighborhood that would have had serious "attitudes" about Laban's trickery. In fact, uncle Laban would have ended up with some missing teeth! Of course, Jacob was shocked, disappointed and probably furious toward his uncle. **Sound familiar?** Perhaps older brother Esau experienced the same roller-coaster of emotions when he discovered brother Jacob tricked dear old dad Isaac into giving the cherished blessing to Jacob, which rightfully belonged to Esau. Does this sound a little like a modern-day soap opera? I think so.

Spiritual Point:

God may forgive us of wrongdoing but we do not necessarily escape all consequences. As Jacob tricked Esau, he later became the object of an elaborately planned trick!

Laban prepared in advance for Jacob's outrage. Seemingly, he had calculated Jacob's actions and reactions (which tell us Laban wasn't sorry for the deception). Laban proceeds to cajole and calm Jacob by promising that once Leah's wedding week was completed, Jacob could still have Rachel whom he truly desired. In return however, Laban proposed that Jacob work *an additional 7 long years. Whaaat?!* And guess what? Jacob did just that (Genesis 29:28).

Bless his heart, Jacob ended up with 2 wives and two maid servants (Zilpah and Bilhah), which came with his wives.

Okay, right about now, let me "play the devil's advocate". There are a couple very small, personal questions, nagging at me: i.e., how did Jacob spend an entire night with a woman who was <u>not Rachel</u>? *Hello??* When a man is so much in love, and has courted or romanced his fiancé over several years, how did Jacob <u>not realize</u> somebody was in his bed, other than Rachel??

Was it too much champagne perhaps? Strong wine, good music, and the anticipation of a long-awaited marriage night could possibly have dulled Jacob's senses. Pause and discuss.

<u>Reflections:</u>

What convinced Jacob to commit to another 7 years of labor with somebody who clearly did not have an ethical bone in his body? Laban was a proven manipulator. Was it Jacob's sense of honor or his intense lust for Rachel? Or could it have been the unresolved estrangement (back home) between him and Esau, which convinced Jacob to delay returning home?

Chapter 4

Being a romantic myself, one of the scriptures that touched my heart is Genesis 29:31, "when the Lord saw that **Leah** was unloved, he opened her womb, but Rachel was barren." This is a revealing insight into the depth of God's compassion and tenderness toward women. Until then, the Genesis passage is pretty much about Jacob's family and his predicament. We watch him being attracted to Laban's younger daughter, requesting her hand in marriage almost immediately. We see how Jacob (in spite of his sense of entitlement), was eventually "played for a fool" and lured into marrying

Rachel's sister whom he had absolutely no desire for at all! However, God was observing all things. God protected Jacob and tenderly watched over Leah; innocent Leah who would become a pillar of faith and fortitude within the lineage of Jesus.

Pause and Pray:

Consider the folks who have rejected, ignored underestimated or manipulated you. Pray for their hearts to turn away from valuing their own needs over how God instructs us to treat each other. Pray God's mercy toward them. Sisters, a clear sign of spiritual growth is when you can sincerely pray for another who has wronged you. How do you grade yourself on this ability?

Again, join me please in a close and loving look at our sister *Leah,* our "shero". She was older sister, the one hovering in the background, mistreated, disrespected and unappreciated by blood relatives. Leah, was labeled weak-eyed and possibly so unattractive that finding a husband for her was something her own father deemed troublesome. Since their tradition was for the oldest daughter to marry first, Laban must have <u>previously</u> tried to secure a husband for Leah. Perhaps possible suitors were "turned off" by her physical imperfection, so when Jacob wanted to marry the younger girl, Laban seized the perfect chance to "hustle up a husband for Leah". I will personally *admit* to occasionally feeling unattractive in a world which promotes a very narrow definition of "beauty" and "desirable". How about you my sisters?

<u>Reflections:</u>

Do you think Leah <u>desired</u> a husband? What emotions do you think she experienced once her own father declared she must participate in deceiving Jacob? Did Leah have the ability to actually refuse her father's plan?

Disappointment is common in everyday life. Have you ever been taken advantage of, put in a situation where you felt you had no control, accompanied by emotions of insult and humiliation? Well, that's how Leah began her life as Jacob's wife. Can you imagine hearing the outrage and <u>disgust</u> in Jacob's voice once he sobered up, woke up and discovered the woman he consummated his marriage with, was in fact....the "ugly duckling" rather than the "swan" he felt entitled to? From that point on, Leah lived daily with wounded emotions, obviously resulting from her being :

- a) manipulated by her father,
- b) undesired by her husband, and
- c) the object of resentment from her sister (Genesis 30:1)

<u>Pause and Pray:</u>
Identify a circumstance or person who insulted you based solely on your imperfect physical appearance or lack of ability. If you identify with Leah's hurts, pray for the Holy Spirit to *remove*

that painful memory and any lingering bitterness. The more I study scriptures, the more I'm reminded how little time Christians invest in communicating with the Holy Spirit. I've mentioned that the Holy Spirit was sent to perform <u>several</u> functions within a Christian's life. Women should acknowledge the Holy Spirit's presence within our devotion time and <u>regularly</u> invite him to reveal sensitive areas that need healing.

From scriptures, we can glean that Leah cared deeply for Jacob and repeatedly tried to please him. Could it be that while Jacob was yearning for Rachel, Leah was 'carrying a torch' for the handsome Jacob? I believe Leah, being the oldest, <u>definitely wanted</u> a husband. She craved to be a wife and bear children; to finally 'fit in' with her peers in the community. After being teased and passed over due to other's perception that she was 'blemished', Leah ached to feel significant and secure within herself and her environment. Inside <u>all of us</u> is the need for validation and acceptance. Those are basic emotional needs for all humans. God, the original designer, made us in him image, right?

We were crafted with those longings because God's original intent was for us to crave <u>Him.</u> Unfortunately, if acceptance is withheld long enough, many women are emotionally driven to fill that longing elsewhere.

<u>Reflection/Discussion:</u>
What do you feel about a <u>woman's longing</u> referred to in Genesis 3:16? "To the woman (God said): I will greatly increase your pains in childbearing; with pain you will give birth to children. Your desire will be for your husband, and he will rule over you." That scripture alludes to a New Testament passage which reads: "Now I want you to realize that the head of every man is Christ, and the head of every

woman is man, and the head of Christ is God." (I Corinthians 11:3)

I realize many women in today's society may take serious objection to those statements; however, I believe that women, then and now, have an innate compulsion which drives us to please our mates and others we need acceptance from. I said it, yes I did! The sooner we understand the truth about our unmet needs, the sooner we can regain emotional stability. The attachment we feel to our significant others and the loyalty we invest into relationships began in the Garden. God was not pleased with the disobedience of Adam and Eve. They were given all they needed for a peaceful life. Yet, they erred by listening to a strange voice (the serpent). After listening, they <u>doubted the truth of God's instructions!</u> Since Adam listened to Eve (and ate the fruit), God purposely placed a compulsion within us women to desire our husband/loved one's approval. There is a great sermon in that sentence, but let's continue.

Spiritual Points

Your own past could possibly hold an unresolved issue(s) of being accepted. Many of us have "jumped through hoops" to win praise or recognition from someone or perhaps tried desperately to 'blend in' with a social club, group of co-workers, etc. Be honest. Next, apologize specifically to the Holy Spirit for not viewing yourself as God has always viewed you; fearfully and wonderfully made (Psalm 139:14).

Pause and pray:

Identify the time(s) you doubted you were good enough, pretty enough or smart enough. Ask for forgiveness for doubting and not appreciating God's workmanship within you. <u>Decide</u> to accept how God has designed you. Now, pray the victory over negative, hindering thoughts. Cast them from your mind, knowing that our divine Creator considers you valuable!

Once a woman believes her family or God values her <u>less than another person,</u> she has slipped into self-deception and low self-image, resulting in <u>discouragement</u> which is one of Satan's greatest weapons! The craving to be significant can become a long-term emotional trap (especially for women who have experienced abuse, neglect or abandonment) and can impact the next generation. While vulnerable, we tend to gravitate toward friends and unhealthy <u>intimate relationships</u> which lure us in with a pretense of "happiness". We may cling to one or more person, place or thing which makes us <u>feel needed.</u> Often, as in my own life years ago, we'll continue trying to <u>earn or win recognition, love and loyalty</u> (blinded to the fact that those people have no intention of giving love and loyalty in return!)

Repeated situations like this will result in spiritual "strongholds" and emotional addictions. Most addictions originate from our attempt to meet a legitimate need in an illegitimate manner. If you have heard the phrase 'stronghold' yet are not clear what it means: a stronghold is any seductive, faulty, deceptive mindset or behavior... that <u>holds you strong and obstructs the flow of God's power and peace into your life!</u>

Strongholds were the cornerstones of Leah's interaction with men for a long time. First, she was a disappointment to her father Laban (being born a female when in biblical times, fathers prayed for sons). Secondly, Leah was born with a physical imperfection which sparked a challenge in securing a husband. So, Leah retreated to a safe place (she thought) within her family's heart. In return, Laban through hard-working Jacob, seized an opportunity to lift his own prestige in the community. Through deception, he married Leah off first. He traded his own daughter like a piece of property, unconcerned about her wounded pride and future humiliation. Recovering from this type of emotional upheaval can be a long, tedious process. The process begins when a woman is exposed to God's word, <u>believes</u> His promises (over her emotions) and truly surrenders <u>anything</u> which hinders her peace of mind (Romans 12: 1-2).

Reflections/Discussion

Do you see the common ground between Rebekah and Laban? Is it possible for us to be sympathetic toward Laban at all? Yes, he knew Jacob really was in love with Rachel. However, could Laban have been wise enough to believe that Jacob would <u>take care of Leah</u> and not treat her poorly (since they were blood relatives)?

Chapter 5

In Genesis 28:1-9, Jacob's brother Esau went through his own hurt pride and feelings of being cast away. After Jacob journeyed to Laban's home in Paddam-Aram, Esau <u>correctly evaluated</u> how much his marrying Canaanite women had grieved his parents. He went to his uncle Ishmael (the son of Abraham and the Egyptian Hagar), and took Ishmael's daughter to be his third wife. That major decision seems indicative of Esau's need to reconnect. I believe he either wanted to "get in good standing" again or he genuinely <u>repented</u> (felt godly sorrow) for his rebellion toward his parents.

Spiritual Point:

Throughout scriptures we learn that when we confess our sins, God is faithful and just to forgive our sins, and to cleanse us from unrighteousness. Locate passages in the Old and New Testaments which clarify God showing compassion on his people when they acknowledge and <u>turn from living against his commands.</u>

Picking up our story in Genesis 29, after the shock had subsided, Jacob stays with Laban, his 2 wives and 2 servants an additional 7 years. It is probably safe to say Jacob was not an overly aggressive personality. He decided to make the most of the commitment he had made. I pause here to point out, that after all his declarations of love for Rachel, if Jacob didn't love <u>Leah, why did he continue having intimate times with her?</u>

I present these possibilities. Jacob didn't honor Leah initially. Leah was deeply grieved, yet continued doing "her best in a bad situation". Leah probably spent many nights alone, sick at heart because her lawful husband spent so much time with her younger, more beautiful sister. Leah continued to <u>honor her husband.</u> By honoring Jacob she blessed God. Consider 1 Peter 3: 3-5, 6b:

"Your beauty should not come from outward adornment, such as braided hair and

the wearing of gold jewelry and fine clothes. Instead, it should be that of your inner self, the unfading beauty of a gentle and quiet spirit, which is of great worth in God's sight. For this is the way the <u>holy women</u> of the past who put their hope in God used to make themselves beautiful. They were submissive to their own husbands. (6b)You are her daughters if you do what is right and do not give way to fear."

Because of her faith and gentleness, at some point, Jacob must have shared the story of how Isaac had blessed him and prophesied that many nations would emerge from Jacob's bloodline. I believe Leah began humbling her heart toward Jacob's God. Perhaps she became an intercessor in those late night hours! God looked upon Leah with compassion because He recognized her love was pure, without ulterior motive.

Our sister Leah must have possessed an attitude of optimism, don't you agree? How else could she have withstood such an emotional roller coaster?

Reflections

Leah was very wise in deciding not to resolve her marital stress through <u>her own strength.</u> As new covenant women, what can you and I now learn from her example about relationships we are drawn to, yet leave us so unfulfilled?

I urge you to examine Romans 5:1-5. "*We have peace with God through our Lord Jesus Christ, through whom we have gained access by faith into this grace in which we now stand. And we rejoice in the hope of the glory of God. Not only so, but we also rejoice in our sufferings, because we know that suffering produces perseverance; perseverance, character; and character, hope. And hope does not disappoint us, because God* *has <u>poured out his love into our hearts</u> by the Holy Spirit, whom he has given us."*

    While Leah hoped her family would love and validate her, we can know for certain that no matter how others interact with us, we have a <u>divine</u> love poured into us. We have a constant, secure hope. He never disappoints.

<u>Pause and Pray</u>

    Take a few moments, pray and journal below how the truth of Romans 5:1-5 speaks to your spirit.

Scriptures teach us that we have weapons of warfare, <u>spiritual</u> weapons at our disposal, and they are *mighty*. Whenever you feel overwhelmed by circumstances you cannot alter, <u>resist your initial emotional response</u>. Pray, practice some calming techniques, and <u>listen</u> for the Holy Spirit who will speak back saying:

    a) We have the weapon of prayer

b) We have the weapon of love
(2 Corinthians 2:13)
c) We have the name of Jesus as a weapon
d) We have the weapon of fervent praise and worship
e) We have the weapon of faith (since our weapons have divine power) and
f) We have the anointing, (ability) to demolish arguments and cast down <u>each</u> disobedient *thought* which exalts itself over what we have learned about God (2 Corinthians 10:4-5).

<u>Reflection:</u>

I have a hard-working church friend named Gloria. In her career, just as she was at the brink of retirement, her employer altered the company policy, pressuring Gloria and several other 'tenured' employees, to either accept early retirement or transfer to brand new positions which meant relocation. Can you *imagine* the surprise, bewilderment and frustration Gloria felt?

List two other emotions which may have been *harder for her to describe:*

_____ *and* _____.

In reflecting on Rachel, we can only guess the *hurt* and maybe bitterness she harbored. Yes, Jacob chose her first, but in reality, Leah was his first wife, the legal "first lady". It's possible that since Rachel could not retaliate against Laban, Rachel took out her anger on Leah and <u>maybe on Jacob also.</u> During those nights when Jacob entered Rachel's tent, perhaps her insecurities prompted her to nag and provoke Jacob. You know what I mean ladies, with questions like: "Is my skin softer than Leah's? Who pleases you more? Do you kiss her the <u>same way</u> you kiss and caress me?"

Now tell the truth sisters....have you ever loved someone who <u>you knew for certain</u> had another love interest? How did you cope? Did the relationship grow stronger or weaker?

What if Leah's humility, kindness and patience eventually penetrated Jacob's heart? She was aware of her physical shortcomings, but she persevered and consequently built up "her inner woman". Leah focused on cultivating her gentle, quiet spirit which is the beauty <u>God treasures.</u> Sisters, some of us have survived several emotional upheavals in spite of two strong weapons of Satan. Those two weapons are:

Disillusionment and discouragement.

<u>Strategies for beating back disillusionment and discouragement:</u>
a. Check out that woman in your mirror.....and tell her the truth (Matthew 22:37). Have you made God your first love, or does he have a low priority?
b. Be <u>vigilant</u> to correct <u>your own</u> ungodly thoughts and behaviors (Galatians 5: 22-26),

c. Get acquainted with virtuous women of scripture (Proverbs 31),

d. Purposely expand your environment (make new friends, set new goals, increase intellect),

e. Take your dream off "the back burner" and shine some light on it. Commit it back to God with renewed zeal, believing the Holy Spirit will complete the 'good work' of your heart and hands, and

f. Purposely restrict and re-channel sexual energy especially unmarried ladies, (Colossians 3:5-6).

Peace Point:

Sisters, don't be deceived. God does not tempt his people with evil. Satan does. We live in a society where sexual, lustful images are common. The Bible is not out of date, for it reads, "temptation *is common* to man; yet, we have divine help....." And God is faithful; he will not let you be tempted beyond what you can bear. But when you are tempted, He will also provide a way of escape so that you can stand up under it." (I

Corinthians 10:13) Now those are *two* mighty powerful promises! So, what preventive actions can <u>you</u> take to filter out temptations?

Let me share a true story with you. In my younger years, I had a strong affinity to nice looking guys. Okay, actually I <u>loved, admired and lusted for extremely handsome, gorgeous men.</u> I can share this now because the shame is gone. Now there was one popular man that I had seen on television several times. He was so handsome that I would fantasize about having his arms wrapped around me. Understand that I have never met the man. If he actually met me today and heard this story, he'd probably be embarrassed. Did I mention that he is a Minister? Anyway, because watching that handsome man on television.... became a *<u>distraction</u>* for me, a potential weakness, I confessed my thoughts and then....I turned the channel! We <u>always</u> have options my sisters, we always have a choice. You do not have to *burn with desire* just because desire rises up. If you already know someone or someplace is a weak area for you, pray for discipline and <u>put precautions in place.</u> We can yield to temptation or we can resist it <u>before</u> it has a chance to entice us into something worse.

Ultimately, Leah's decision to do the right thing for the right reason propelled her into a

prominent place. She was Jacob's first wife and she matured into that role by developing her own spiritual life. I believe she had a kind and generous spirit; well respected among her peers. She's actually one of our unheralded role models.

We should applaud the godly example she set. Deception and manipulation were imbedded into Leah's wedding night. Yet, no matter how loveless her marriage may have begun, through her prayers she adorned herself with patience and wisdom. Those virtues elevated her smack into a place we must all strive for: *right in the midst of our Lord's divine will.*

Chapter 6

There is no scriptural evidence that Jacob was cruel toward Leah, or ever physically mistreated her (another example of God's compassion). In fact, I'm quite confident believing that while Jacob initially desired Rachel <u>only</u>, because Leah consistently demonstrated she was a devoted wife and mother, he grew extremely fond of her.

The facts speak for themselves. I image during the long, cold winters and many hot, summer nights, Leah clung desperately to Jacob, whispering her own loyalty to him. Jacob's intimacy with Leah blossomed. They parented not just one child but *6 sons and 1 daughter.* Just like women today, Leah encountered storms of life, yet as she prayed and trusted her way through, she experienced small successes, which ultimately resulted into bountiful blessings.

It is essential we spend some time exploring Leah's childbearing years. From her words and experiences we glean how Leah's spiritual life flourished, just as God planned.

Spiritual Point:
As a redeemed child of God, always remember: Nothing happens outside his permissive will. Our comfort must be that since God allows our circumstances......*there must be a purpose for them.*

It has been said that each person in our life is either God-sent or God- used. *Actually, he already knew we would survive what we survived.* Because He is God!

Motherhood, during Old Testament times held great significance. Whenever a son was born, not only was the father held in high esteem, but the status of the *mother* and the entire family was elevated.

Scripture leaves no doubt as to why Leah bore a son first:

"*The Lord saw that Leah was unloved.*" (Genesis 29:31)

No matter how many times I read that verse, I still envision almighty God actually hanging over the balcony of Heaven, observing how his chosen vessel was being treated. <u>*If the Lord saw Leah then, He sees you and me now.*</u> *He cares.*

"The Lord is <u>near</u> to those who have a broken heart, and saves such as has a contrite spirit. Many are the afflictions of the righteous, but the Lord delivers him/her out of them all." (Psalm 34:18-19). That's good news!

Reflections

Who or what has broken your heart that you were convinced would value you? How do you remember the Lord softening your pain? Loving ourselves and seeing ourselves as God does is very hard work. Have you ever felt God was not interested in your concerns and hurts? Confess your doubts and meditate on the scripture above. <u>Decide to trust</u> the word of God to nourish and heal your heart.

Can you speak of times when you were sure nobody but God orchestrated a blessing just for you? Of course He did, because he knows all that threatens or harms us. "Behold the eye of the Lord is on those who fear Him, on those who <u>hope</u> in His mercy". (Psalm 33:18) We must not doubt where our hope and help comes from my sisters. Because God saw Leah's anguish due to her "unloved state"; because she desired to honor Him and her husband, God opened Leah's womb.

She gave birth to their first son, <u>Reuben.</u> She exclaimed (Gen. 29:32), "Behold, a son! The Lord has surely looked on my affliction. Now therefore, my husband will love me." Reuben represented Leah's unmet need for validation and love, mingled with astonishment at God's kindness and compassion toward her. Can you imagine how tenderly she held that child, how tears must have trickled down Leah's cheeks as she rocked baby Reuben to sleep? She's holding the proof God has not forgotten her!

However, in her everyday reality, her husband still cleaved to the true love of his heart, Rachel. Leah hoped giving birth to their second son, <u>Simeon,</u> would win over Jacob's heart. Yet, after bearing another son, her celebratory time was overshadowed. "Yes, I have birthed two sons" she probably reasoned, "yet my joy isn't complete because my husband is still sharing a marriage bed with my sister."

<u>Reflections:</u>

Can you identify Leah's unmet needs or struggles? Can you write at least three?

_____

_____ _____

If you are currently experiencing one or more of the needs you just listed; <u>pause and earnestly pray</u> for strength to forgive <u>any</u> person, <u>any</u> situation or condition which contributed to your unmet needs. Invite the cleansing, healing power of the Holy Spirit into your heart and mind. As a born again believer, you have the authority and the right to do so.

At any time, have you tried to sustain a neglectful or emotionally draining marriage, friendship or other relationship.....hoping against hope that "a change is going to come"? If so, write down what you were <u>waiting for</u> during that period. What about friends or loved ones you "broke up with", yet took them back <u>more than once</u>, only to have them betray your friendship or trust *<u>again?</u>*

Chapter 7

What compels some women to try-and-try-and-try again, with the *same* man who has displayed a lack of commitment more than once?

Unfortunately, rather than a simple answer, there is usually a multi-layered explanation which seems illogical to persons with strong self-esteem. Therapists and counselors use the term "codependency". To put it simply, most women "love deeply" and "love long." I'm familiar with a woman, Lynn. Her mother died after birthing 6 children. Lynn was then raised by her dad and older sister. She was a nice looking lady, a meticulous house keeper with a good sense of humor. She graduated from high school but never went further, preferring to get a factory job and help her father raise the family.

Lynn's father was a very likeable man, but much of his leisure time was spent with his fraternity activities and his drinking friends, rather than doing homework and nurturing his daughters. He did however, spend a good deal of time with his <u>sons</u>.

Lynn grew up believing it was normal to work all week and head to a club or community dance for recreation on Fridays & Saturdays. Can you guess the type of guys Lynn was attracted to? Mostly men who patronized clubs, gambled, danced well talked loud and drank....a lot. Lynn fell in love with a man who drank and eventually beat her up for complaining about his behavior. Her next lover became the father of her two children. They were together several years while he served in the Air Force. She tried hard to establish a comfortable home and she was a good mother. Eventually, her boyfriend's emotional and physical abuse caused her to leave that city and return to her hometown.

She tried dating older men, younger men, and finally became attached to a man who had a very stable job, his own house, yet one main flaw. He was an alcoholic, and miserable. As her frustrations increased, unfortunately Lynn's mild manner turned to agitation and verbal abuse toward her own children. As I tried to encourage Lynn to recognize the 'warning signs', and cut her losses with this current relationship, she decided to give him "one more chance". *Sound familiar?* To sum up, Lynn stayed with the last alcoholic for 14 years! Was the boyfriend the core problem? Not entirely. More than that, her faulty belief system about male and female "roles" restricted Lynn from establishing <u>safe</u> boundaries for herself <u>and for her children.</u>

<u>Point to ponder:</u>

Ladies, let me share a hard-learned secret about relationships. The person who is <u>least</u> invested emotionally, will usually dominate the relationship. *Why?* Because they are not willing to compromise. Any man, or any person who exhibits a self-centered mindset, will <u>allow</u> you to frustrate <u>yourself</u>....*trying to change them.*

That is a sad but true insight. This happens not just within marriages, but in friendships, among co-workers and with relatives who ignore your suggestions and sound advice. You keep trying to "bring out the potential you see in them". Why will women strive to correct a lopsided relationship with men who don't make the same effort? The fear of being alone is a huge influence. Also, we are driven to not have another relationship <u>end in failure.</u>

I'll share a personal example with you. During the 1980's I dated a man with an established reputation as a "player". Let's call him Eric. Well, I set my mind on winning his heart, but with one drawback: he never intended to fall in love with me or offer anything more than physical encounters. He was "the life of the party" yet could be egotistical and often untruthful (Sisters, do not minimize those warning signs). Yes, our intimate times were fantastic and he actually grew very fond of me. Eric however, continued to introduce me to everybody as his friend. Me, I was completely over my head in a one-sided attachment. I defended him to my friends. Months later, after a minor disagreement, he "dropped me like a hot potato" and relocated out of state soon after. I was devastated. I may have found some comfort if he had chosen another *woman* (but that's another story for another day).   Over time, I realized God had allowed that experience to teach me to seek His will first. He continued to show favor on me while Eric's lifestyle failed to prosper him.

As we rejoin Sister Leah, it is important that we chart her spiritual journey through her "birthing phases". Let's remember that Leah

began marriage and motherhood with a consuming belief that she must seek love and acceptance from another human being (her husband). Genesis 29:34 states she birthed a third son, Levi. With a yearning heart, Leah declared, "Now at last my husband will become attached to me, because I have borne him three sons." Sadly, Jacob shared his body, yet *still withheld* appreciation and true intimacy from her. Leah's prayer life deepened and slowly, a spiritual awareness matured within her soul.

As Leah conceived again, and birthed a <u>fourth son,</u> she found more strength deep inside herself, and resolutely declared, "This time I will praise the Lord. So she named (her son), Judah." (Genesis 29:34) What happened? She changed her mind! Leah stopped counting her losses and started counting her blessings. She realigned her thoughts which raised her self-appreciation. Leah recognized she was *indeed* loved and favored by her husband's God. When a woman changes her perspective, she regains power, praise God! Let me share another revelation: Relinquishing your <u>need</u> to be the main object of another person's affection or adoration is an effective method for correcting faulty thinking (especially for women in unfulfilling relationships).

Revisit Romans Chapter 12 please. This chapter urges us to offer our bodies 'as living sacrifices, holy and pleasing <u>to God</u>, not other humans! We are not to conform to the world's pattern (of thinking and behaving) but we are to be <u>transformed by renewing our minds.</u>

A few pages ago, I mentioned a term "codependency", which is a real disorder first identified back in the 1950s. It carries a wide array of emotional peaks and valleys, wreaking havoc in the lives of many, wives, mothers, girlfriends, even grandmothers of all ages. I am a <u>survivor</u> of that disorder. Initially you feel that you are called to make somebody else's life better. Gradually and with the best intentions, there is a realization of becoming unsettled, confused in your thinking. You lower your boundaries and begin putting up with behaviors which you previously would not tolerate. Codependency is an unhealthy attachment to people and their wellbeing, to such an extent that you put your own emotional and/or physical health at risk. Co-dependency is <u>not love</u>. At its worse, it resembles addiction. Keep reading, I'll return to that point.

Sister Leah has finally, after the birth of Judah, emerged from the kind of despair many people can only imagine. Another author compared Judah's birth (Judah means 'praise'), to the completion of a rainbow in Leah's life. What allowed her to give praise was Leah finally being submitted to the Lord's will. Submission resulted in an emotional victory over her circumstances. She no longer viewed herself as a helpless *victim*. She stopped chasing after and yearning after Jacob's love and learned how to <u>rest</u> in God's demonstrated love. That's where God always wanted women to be, resting in Him. I believe that's truly when we "get our groove back".

Leah had much more strength than she originally believed. And so do you my sister! You may have encountered some fierce storms of financial depletion, failure in relationships, unfulfilled dreams, just as Leah encountered.

Her father mistreated and manipulated her. She endured her husband's disgust and cold rejection, compounded with her sister's envy and spite for a long time. Sister Leah lived her personal "crucible". You may ask, what's a crucible?

Chapter 8

A *crucible* (by John Maxwell's definition) is an opportunity, test or emergency that summons the very best of a person and reveals their finest inner qualities. I believe that every time Christians survive a personal crucible, a spiritual transformation occurs. We are never quite so weak, so fearful, so confused again. Yes, we may make another bad emotional decision; however, we can refer back to the previous obstacle we survived with God's grace. Knowing that God was previously with us gives us a confidence, a faith in the substance of things we hope for; the evidence of things not yet seen. Yeah!

Not-so-pretty, weak-eyed, unloved Leah birthed the leader of the tribe of Judah, from which our Savior emerged. She stayed meek, upheld her position and demonstrated self-respect. Her humility and loving heart allowed God to do a mighty work <u>in Leah</u>.....and *through Leah.* For a time, she ceased having children personally, yet Jacob fathered other children through Rachel's maid Bilhah, *and <u>Leah's maid Zilpah.</u>* Now sisters, don't get it twisted. God allowed all this to occur through his permissive will, yet Leah remained "the first wife". More often than not, we hear from television and gossip tabloids when a celebrity's infidelity is discovered, right? Well, Leah knew right from day one that her husband had another lover, that he even <u>preferred</u> being with Rachel. So how could Leah stay *sane,* knowing her husband was intimate with two other women in addition to her sister Rachel? She kept her sanity by taking Jacob off a pedestal and putting God on a pedestal.

By the time Leah birth her fourth son Judah, Rachel was absorbed with her own jealousy and feelings of inferiority. Genesis Chapter 30:1 records Rachel's outburst to Jacob, "give me children, or I'll die!"

Spiritual Point

What insight do we get about Rachel from her comments? Briefly summarize her:

a) emotional state, and

b) her spiritual state

Allow me to share a quote which grabbed my attention: *"Falling in love is a temporary madness; it erupts in your soul and then subsides.*

Life itself is what's left once the sensation of falling in love has subsided. Remember to bring the wood in before she asks you. If she is cold, put a shawl around her shoulders, and bring her a flower every time you return from the fields."
(From movie: Captain Corelli's Mandolin).

You see, Rachel and Jacob fell into love pretty quick (perhaps sparked by lust). Leah <u>grew into love,</u> first with her husband and then with his God. That's pretty powerful. On the other hand, once the children began to come, <u>Rachel's</u> expectations were profoundly shattered. Her self-confidence had hung on the hope that she'd also birth sons by Jacob. When our emotional expectations and needs are not met, disappointment and frustration are usually our first reactions. Resentment and anger don't lag too far behind. Gone was the complete abandon Rachel felt when Jacob held her close. This was now *real life* and she felt like a fool. The unattractive Leah got to have the babies, why not Rachel? It must be Jacob's fault. She never considered that God could have been displeased with *her* behavior. It took a while for pretty Rachel to re-adjust her attitude. Can you relate in any way?

Now notice in Chapter 30: 2-6, how Rachel decided, like Sarah had with Abraham, to create her "family" by suggesting a surrogate to Jacob. Initially, Jacob really "put Rachel in her place". He told her straight up that he was not in the place of God "who has kept you from having children". But then he calmed down and went to have consensual sex with their maid Bilhah. Could you have done the same? Now don't say no too quickly because right now, there are many women who are "sharing their men". They just may not know the *other woman's name.* You may know or have known a lady who slipped around with a married man. With Leah and Rachel, Jacob's partners were no secret.

Was God giving a nod of approval in this?

Reflections:

Sisters, let's pause a moment and put husband Jacob "on the hot seat". Am I the only one who notices how easily led that man was? Remember while he still lived with his parents, Jacob retracted when faced with a strong-willed woman. His mother Rebekah initiated the plan for Jacob to deceive Isaac by pretending to be his older brother Esau. Jacob expressed one feeble concern, then did exactly what he <u>knew</u> was wrong (Genesis 27). Now, here he is arguing with the wife he adores, *Rachel.* He is correct in saying her barrenness is not <u>his fault.</u> Yet, at Rachel's insistence, Jacob has intercourse with Bilhah, making Rachel's servant his sexual surrogate. Why couldn't Jacob, as the family leader, have the fortitude to "just say no" to Rachel? I believe he repeated the patterns of his core family. With both his mother and wife, Jacob retreated from confrontation. Was his behavior out of respect or perhaps from another motive? Realizing the husband is to be prophet, priest and protector of the family, did Jacob exhibit a character flaw? Pause and discuss.

    We must again recognize how these women found deep significance within childbearing. It is a reality that women *were* considered *property* many times throughout scripture. However, a central belief about themselves hung on their ability to procreate. That's another reason it is critical for us to know the Lord *first*. When our understanding of Him is strong (through study of scripture) we are freed up to view ourselves through a balanced lens of acceptance and affirmation. I'm fully aware that woman was taken; crafted from man. It's also true that God himself *purposefully* crafted us. We were not an afterthought my sisters. We were tucked inside man until a generous God opened man and lovingly presented woman *as a gift to man.* That is where our authentic identity must begin. So Rachel failed her test. She was driven by her experiences and insecurities which are <u>still</u> inadequate sources toward making wise decisions. Bilhah, on the other hand becomes interwoven into this essential family of our faith. She gives birth to Dan and later to Naphtali (Genesis 30: 8). In her haste, Rachel brags "I've had great struggle with my sister and I have won."

<u>Peace Point:</u>

With Rachel's declaration, which spiritual gift(s) does she lack? (Refer to I Corinthians 13 for help)

Chapter 9

As we press on through Genesis Chapter 30, *Leah* reaches another crucible situation. After her 4th child, there is a long period with no pregnancy. Jacob perhaps is spending more time with Rachel. Then Rachel claims a child for herself through Jacob and Bilhah. Sister Leah, sadly yields to a sense of desperation. Perhaps the long, lonely nights have taken their toll and left her heartbroken. Whatever the logic, Leah, gives <u>her</u> servant Zilpah to Jacob as a sexual surrogate. Why? Some folks would say Leah "stepped up her game" because she didn't have a choice. But there is always a choice. Have you ever done that? Even though the Lord brought you out of a storm, when a new one rises, we often allow a competitive insecurity sparked by fear, to wrap icy fingers around our heart again! *Leah, now in open competition,* stands by as Zilpah bears a son whom Leah named Gad (verse 11). Are you keeping count? Jacob has fathered 7 sons, has 2 regular wives...and 2 sexual servant- wives! Wow. Then comes Asher, the 8th son fathered by Jacob, birthed by Zilpah.

Sisters, we already *have power!* We don't have to compete or manipulate anybody to get it. Even after her surrogate children, Rachel is still jealous and resentful of first wife, Leah, and her children who seem to run into blessings. A scene is described where Leah's son Reuben finds some nice mandrake plants which he brings to his mother. Well, Rachel demands a portion of Reuben's mandrakes (Chapter 30: 14). Sister Leah chastises her saying (verse 15); "wasn't it enough that you took away my husband? Will you take my son's mandrakes too?" Just when you think Leah is standing up for herself, Rachel's consuming need <u>for control</u> bursts forth. She rubs salt in Leah's wounds. Displaying her superiority Rachel tells Leah that Jacob has 'permission' to sleep with Leah that night, in return for Reuben's mandrakes! Folks, exactly what were those mandrakes worth? No way, no how, would you have exchanged your husband…or would you? In modern day times, what would serve as "mandrakes"; perhaps a diamond ring, a lavish vacation, a new car with keyless entry, satellite stereo and a built-in GPS system?

And guess what? Our sister Leah, whose spiritual life had matured quite a bit, gave in to Rachel's demand.

Points to Ponder

Along with the disillusionment and discouragement we mentioned earlier, *loneliness* is a powerful enticement, am I right? While Jacob was 'servicing' the two sexual servants and trying to impregnate Rachel, *Leah got ignored again. So she bargained for her husband.*

Loneliness is woven throughout this family and not just in Leah's heart. It is very likely Jacob felt lonely and overlooked years before in a smoldering rivalry for his father Isaac's affection. Then as he rushed away from home and journeyed in the dessert many miles, Jacob experienced lonely, fretful dreams. He wouldn't let go of the visiting angel partly due to wanting all the human contact and blessings he could get. Extending and receiving affection from Rachel lifted his spirits and his ego. Jacob threw himself into Rachel and felt entitled to her. Yet, God allowed an extended delay in her childbearing, I believe, trying to cultivate their <u>character</u>. God works <u>within</u> the free will of each human. We are moral agents for ourselves. God wants our first thoughts <u>and choices</u> to be about pleasing Him. Is it possible Jacob grew comfortable with his "harem", and perhaps gave God a less prominent place in his life?

Can you see any similarities in your life? What are the places, people and things you extend a lot of energy toward? Do you give equal amount of energy to your spiritual development?

How many times monthly does your family see you study God's word or <u>hear your prayers?</u>

I'm asking that question because I realized long after they were grown, that my children didn't see or hear me pray often enough. Yes, we attended church together while they were growing up. However, since their father had periods of incarceration, I was the parent who actually walked in the roles of *prophet, priest, provider, and protector, telling myself that "once he lives up to his potential we'll be a happy family".* Listen closely ladies. The only person you can definitely change is that person in your mirror.

As women, we are compelled to fill several roles within our daily lives. Often after a stressful day, we neglect family prayer & study time. We <u>must carve out</u> significant time for spiritual connection in order to obtain wisdom. Wisdom comes from the study of God's word. Being a disciple means exchanging our flawed will for His perfect will, then <u>living out</u> His teachings. Some good scriptures to encourage you in this area:

Matthew 6:33   *I Chronicles 28:9*

2 Chronicles 7:14   *Luke 18:1*

Matthew 10: 37-39   *Proverbs 3:4-7*

Pray and reflect on the scriptures above. How can you apply those principles into your life?

_____

_____

_____

_____

_____

Chapter 10

Let's return now to Genesis Chapter 30:16. There our sister Leah has exchanged her son's mandrakes for a passionate night with her own husband. When Jacob returned from his workday, Leah met him with a demand wrenched from a heavy heart: *"You must sleep with me. I have hired you with my son's mandrakes."* Sounds to me like an situation of sexual coercion for payment. Hubby Jacob did as he was told. Can you imagine the conversation that night between those two? Did Leah sob silently or was she just resigned to carve out a little happiness for herself? Could you have been content my sister, to share a bed with somebody you loved at any cost?

Even while Leah's emotional roller-coaster continues, she still encounters God's favor. Her words, "God listened to Leah and she bore a 5th son and named him Issachar" are striking. The name Issachar translates "there is a reward". We can assume Leah felt God rewarded her for her commitment. Research states Issachar was born approximately 1746 BC. His offspring developed into a powerful tribe, often numbering over 50,000 fighting warriors.

There is one figure missing in this intriguing family. I see no mention of Leah's and Rachel's mother. We know their father Laban also had sons so it is possible Laban's original wife had died.

Point to ponder

Could Leah's fragile self-esteem have been partly due to being the eldest daughter and not having a consistent, nurturing woman to mentor and advocate for her?   Do you have such a person in your life? If not, how has it impacted you?

Often in current society, there is a noticeable lack of stable, spiritual fathers. In biblical times, fathers filled a strong leadership role (even though Laban was not a great example). But if a compassionate mother was also absent, we are left to wonder who Leah turned to whenever marital drama unfolded. *Pause and pray for any woman you know who must handle adversity without a loving, faith-filled woman to assist her.*

Jacob returns to Leah long enough for her to conceive a 6th son, Zebulum (Genesis 30:19), and one daughter, Dinah (verse 21). After Zebulum's birth, Leah proclaimed, "this time my husband will treat me with honor." Yet, once Dinah was born, the scriptures are silent. No word of joy or promise attached to Dinah. Can you guess why?

I cannot help but mention that finally, in verse 22, "God remembered *Rachel*, he opened her womb". She too became pregnant and gave Jacob another history making son, Joseph.

Clearly, God kept a hedge around this family. From the time Jacob made a vow in the desert of Bethel and built a pillar to God, God was present. Genesis 31 reveals how Laban's attitude toward Jacob changed due to the Jacob's prosperity. The Lord spoke again to Jacob, and finally gave permission for him to return to his own relatives (verse 3). Jacob shared his concerns with Leah and Rachel. They agreed to relocate with their husband. Rachel, however, steals idol gods from her father, confirming once again why the Lord delayed the blessings Rachel felt entitled to (children). Sometimes sisters, we can be our own "blessing blocker". A sure way to reap negative consequences is by becoming absorbed in pride, strife, selfishness, greed and hurtful behaviors toward others.

Pause and Pray

Reflect over some things you feel were withheld from you. Was there possibly a broken ethical standard or a self-serving motive you need to confess?

Of course, Laban pursues Jacob for seven days (Genesis 31:23) and locates him in Gilead. There, the Lord intervenes again and protects Jacob by warning Laban in a dream not to harm him. Laban even accused Jacob of taking the idols. Neither man was aware that the actual thief and liar was Rachel (Genesis 31: 33-35). Rachel never fully gave up her idolatry and felt entitled to steal idols in retaliation for how she felt Laban had wronged them. Her behavior could have resulted in death to family members if Laban had found what he searched for. This was yet another test which sister Rachel, unfortunately failed.

Chapter 11

Much time passes before Dinah, Jacob's only daughter by Leah is mentioned again. After the family settled in Shechem, Dinah is found visiting other women in the community. A man named Shechem, son of a prosperous Hivite ruler, lusted after Dinah. He captured her and sexually molested her. I find it surprising that after the attack (Gen. 34: 1-5), Shechem actually loved Dinah and asked his father to acquire Dinah so they could marry. Jacob decided not to provoke the situation, but several of his sons plotted a deadly revenge due to their sister's dishonor. As you read Genesis Chapters 34 and 35, can you see how Jacob continued to pray and seek God's face? In return, God continued to enlarge Jacob's family (his name was changed to Israel) and lead them through one danger after another.

God promised Israel/Jacob that a nation and community of nations and kings would descend from him (Gen. 35: 9-12). Finally, while Rachel bore her last child Benjamin, she died in childbirth. She was buried on the way to Bethlehem and Israel set a pillar over Rachel's tomb. But what about our sister *Leah?* Israel had already made special provision for her. As he was preparing for his own death, Israel gave his 12 sons his blessing and his instructions. He told his children "bury me with my fathers in the cave in Canaan which Abraham bought as a burial place. There Abraham and Sarah were buried, there Isaac and his wife Rebekah were buried, and there I buried Leah." (Genesis 49:29-31)

Israel chose to spend eternity beside the wife who had shown him unconditional love and devotion. He didn't demand to be next to the wife of his youthful lust, but the wife who had <u>earned</u> his respect through her humble character, loyalty and her personal devotion to God. Although it took many years, Leah achieved the recognition and appreciation for which she longed. She received her rightful place of honor next to the husband she cherished, not by tricks or schemes, but out of pure motives and yielding to God's guidance.

My sisters, my sincere prayer is that you recognize the beauty and uniqueness that our Creator <u>*intentionally deposited within you*</u>. He has known you and designed you with his finger of love. Can you now identify behaviors and thoughts which you can change, to better align your perspective up with God's perspective? He has deposited a *divine* purpose and plan for every woman he created. From this day forward, refuse to "sell yourself short" any longer! You are fearfully and wonderfully made by God, for His purpose and His joy. Love Him first with your whole heart. Then every day, make a decision to *love the Leah in you!*

www.ingramcontent.com/pod-product-compliance
Lightning Source LLC
Chambersburg PA
CBHW031415040426
42444CB00005B/571